SOMERSET

A Celebration of Communities

WALTER CHOROSZEWSKI

Published by

AESTHETIC PRESS, INC.

North Branch, New Jersey

HIGHLAND PARK PUBLIC LIBRARY

SOMERSET, *A Celebration of Communities*

Copyright © 2007 Aesthetic Press, Inc. All rights reserved.
Photography copyright © 2007 Walter Choroszewski. All rights reserved.

No part of this publication may be used or reproduced in any manner whatsoever
without written permission from the publisher, Aesthetic Press, Inc.
Photography may not be used or reproduced in any manner whatsoever
without written permission from the photographer, Walter Choroszewski,
in care of Aesthetic Press, Inc.

ISBN: 1-932803-46-7
First Printing 2007
Printed in Korea

AESTHETIC PRESS, INC.
P.O. Box 5306, North Branch, NJ 08876-1303

Website: www.aestheticpress.com
Email: info@aestheticpress.com
Telephone: (908) 369-3777

SOMERSET
A Celebration of Communities

WALTER CHOROSZEWSKI

▲ *Somerset County Court House (1909), Somerville*

◀◀ *Orchard Drive, Hillsborough*

SOMERSET

FOREWORD *by*

WALTER CHOROSZEWSKI

*F*rom the lush hills of the Highlands to the fertile Coastal Plain, the lands bordering the Raritan River have been inhabited by the Lenape for thousands of years before the first European settlers arrived in the early part of the 17th century.

The etymology of Somerset derives from the Old English term *Sumorsaete*, which meant *"settlers around a summer farmstead."* Named after Somerset in England, locations bearing this name are found in 24 states from Maine to California. One of the oldest is Somerset County, New Jersey, established by Royal Charter in 1688.

Henry Hudson, sailing for the Dutch East India Company in 1609, anchored the *Halve Maen* at the mouth of the Raritan River, but it wasn't until much later that century when settlers ventured up this waterway. The area was then part of New Netherland before the Dutch yielded to English rule in 1664.

Sir George Carteret and Lord Berkeley of Stratton became the new owners of the proprietary colony of "Nova Caesarea" (later known as New Jersey). In 1674 the colony was subdivided into East and West Jersey with border disputes which lasted into the early 18th century. Today's Somerset was located in East Jersey, in the western part of Middlesex County—one of New Jersey's original four counties which were formed in 1675.

Considered to be the first settler in Somerset County, Thomas Codrington, one of the Lords Proprietary of East Jersey, purchased land in 1681. Unlike the other proprietors of this transaction, he was the only one who chose to occupy the land and later built his home near Bound Brook, a small tributary of the Raritan River at the base of the Watchung Mountains.

The Dutch and English continued to acquire lands and build settlements along the Raritan and Millstone Rivers and into the Watchung Hills. Somerset County was then created from rural mountainous portions of Middlesex to become New Jersey's fifth county in 1688. Additional land was added in the early 1700s when the borders of Somerset County were redefined to their present form.

The Lenape were aware of the occasional flooding of the Raritan and its tributaries so they lived on higher ground nearby. The tidal wetlands surrounding the Raritan River reminded the English of a similar landscape of moors and low farmland of Somerset, England. The Raritan River valley, with its fertile savannah-like plains, was ideal for farming.

Throughout the 18th century, roads were built along traditional Lenape pathways as settlers pushed westward, clearing more land for farms and villages and building mills along the waterways. Religious freedom in the colony brought Presbyterian, Dutch Reformed and Congregational churches which were at the center of many villages.

Somerset County was a strategic location during the American Revolution. General Washington passed through the area after his victories in Trenton and Princeton in January of 1777. The Battle of Van Nest Mills (near today's Manville) soon followed and provided another victory for the New Jersey Militia and Pennsylvania "riflemen."

In April of 1777, Lord Charles Cornwallis led 4,000 British and Hessian troops in a surprise attack on Bound Brook, returning to New Brunswick that same evening with many prisoners, cannons and supplies. That defeat at Bound Brook prompted Washington to move his troops to the Watchung Mountains to monitor the British.

Washington's First Encampment at Middlebrook took place through the spring and summer of 1777. With only 8,000 troops, many sick and wounded, he gave the illusion of a much greater force in the Watchungs, thereby disrupting British plans. It was during this encampment that Congress approved the first national flag of the Unites States. The flag was unfurled over the Continental Army for the first time at Middlebrook—an event that is now commemorated each 4th of July.

The winter of 1778-1779 marked the return of the Continental Army to Somerset County. Washington rented the Wallace House in Somerville and General Von Steuben stayed at the Staats House in South Bound Brook, while almost 10,000 Continental troops camped at Middlebrook for a second time.

In October of 1779, British Major John Simcoe and the Queens Rangers, based in New Brunswick, made raids through the county with attacks in Finderne and Somerset Court House (today's Millstone). The British raiders burned a church, the court house and jail before Simcoe was wounded and captured.

Through the balance of the Revolution, Somerset remained in the pathway of other troop movements, encampments and smaller skirmishes. General Washington returned to Rocky Hill in 1783 to stay at "Rockingham," his final headquarters of the war where he authored his Farewell Address to the Army.

The 19th century was a time of prosperity as new transportation routes brought industry and growth to the county. In 1806, the Easton-Brunswick Road (today's Easton Avenue, Routes 28 & 22) was chartered as a toll road and given the name "Jersey Turnpike." The road crossed the county on a northwesterly path to Hunterdon County and Pennsylvania.

The Delaware & Raritan Canal, built in the early 1830s, was a link between the rivers of the same name. Its route paralleled the Millstone and Raritan Rivers along the southern part of the county and was a boon to Rocky Hill, Franklin, Hillsborough, Millstone and South Bound Brook.

The Central Railroad of New Jersey had its origins in Somerset County with the Elizabethtown and Somerville Railroad, chartered in 1831. A westward rail connection, the Somerville and Easton Railroad, was built in the 1840s and a southwestern route to Flemington was made by the South Branch Railroad in the 1860s. The New Jersey West Line Railroad brought service to the northern towns of Somerset Hills in the 1870s. All of the county's railroad towns flourished as town centers developed around the stations.

With the advent of the automobile, a highway system was developed which again placed Somerset County in the crossroads. One of the first highways in America was U.S. Route 22—a Blue-Star Memorial Highway. It was built in 1926 connecting New Jersey and Ohio and crossed Somerset in an east-west direction incorporating some existing routes in the county. The following year Route 28 evolved from an old alignment of Route 22. In the 1930s, U.S. Highway 202—stretching from Maine to Delaware—traversed the county from Bernardsville to Branchburg. State Highway 206 was finalized in 1953 as a north-south highway which ran from Peapack-Gladstone to Montgomery.

In 1956 President Eisenhower created the Interstate Highway System. New Jersey was already quite developed and residents gave opposition and resistance to the proposed routes of the highways. Almost fifty years later, Route 78 was finally completed as a major pathway to New York City, crossing Bedminster, Bridgewater, Warren and Watchung. Interstate 287 (the Middlesex Freeway) was built as a New York City beltway which hugged the Watchung Ridge and intersected with Route 78 in Bedminster.

The highways of the 20th century brought many new residents to Somerset County. Its population grew tenfold from approximately 30,000 in 1900, to over 300,000 today. Many farms were lost to this suburban development. Much of Somerset's manufacturing which flourished in New Jersey's Golden Age of Industry has now been replaced by corporations and retail centers. Somerset County had been home to numerous corporate headquarters and is now renowned as a center for biotechnology and pharmaceutical industry.

In the face of this growth which continues into the 21st century, Somerset County has been strong in its preservation efforts with almost 10,000 acres of parkland and over 5,000 acres of preserved farmland. Historic sites, buildings and monuments, celebrating the county's rich colonial and Revolutionary heritage, are found in almost every municipality. Somerset County is comprised of suburban and rural areas with amenities and a lifestyle which often rank it as one of the top locations in America.

Author's Note:

*My family and I have made Somerset County our home since 1985. I find that the county has changed dramatically in the years since my 1999 book, **SOMERSET COUNTY, A Millennial Portrait**. Revisiting all of its towns has yielded many new discoveries and has reaffirmed my appreciation for Somerset. I hope you enjoy and share in my passion for the county's scenic beauty, rich history and people in **SOMERSET, A Celebration of Communities**.*

Bedminster Township

The Township of Bedminster was officially created by Royal Charter in 1749 and later incorporated in 1798. Scots-Irish, German and Dutch settlers probably arrived in the early 1700s and built farms and mills north of the Lamington and North Branch Raritan Rivers. They established The Presbyterian Church at Lamington in 1741. Quaint historic villages dot a rural landscape known for its horse farms and estates. Positioned at the base of Schley Mountain, near the crossroads of Routes 78, 287, 202 and 206, the village of Pluckemin, with a rich Revolutionary War history, is the economic and populous center of the township.

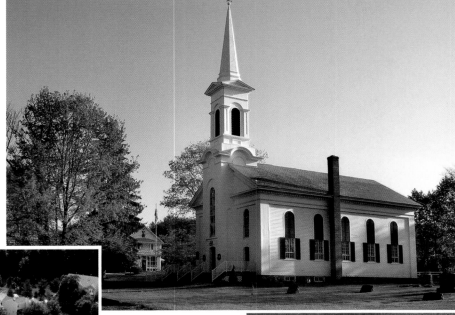
▲ *Pottersville Reformed Church (1855)*

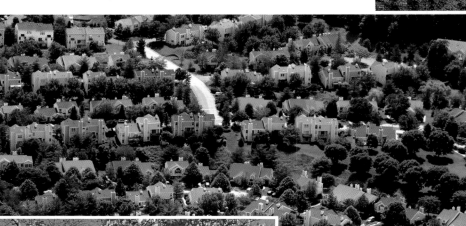
▼ *Jacobus Vanderveer House (1770s)*

▲ *Aerial (The Hills)*

▼ *Sign, Bedminster Township School*

▲ *Lamington Presbyterian Church Cemetery*

Horse farm, Rattlesnake Bridge Road

Lamington Greenway, Rattlesnake Bridge Road

National Cancer Survivors Day
Red Balloon Celebration
& Ice Cream Social,
The Wellness Community of Central New Jersey,
Burnt Mills Road

Collecting Gaits Farm / USEF Dressage Festival of Champions

16 A

Somerset Art Association,
Burnt Mills Road

Upper Raritan Watershed Association Annual Dinner, Hamilton Farm Golf Club

▲ *Upper Raritan Watershed Association Gardens at Fairview Farms*

▶ *Lamington Road*

▲ *Larger Cross Road*

▲ *Burnt Mills Road*

▶ *Burnt Mills Road*

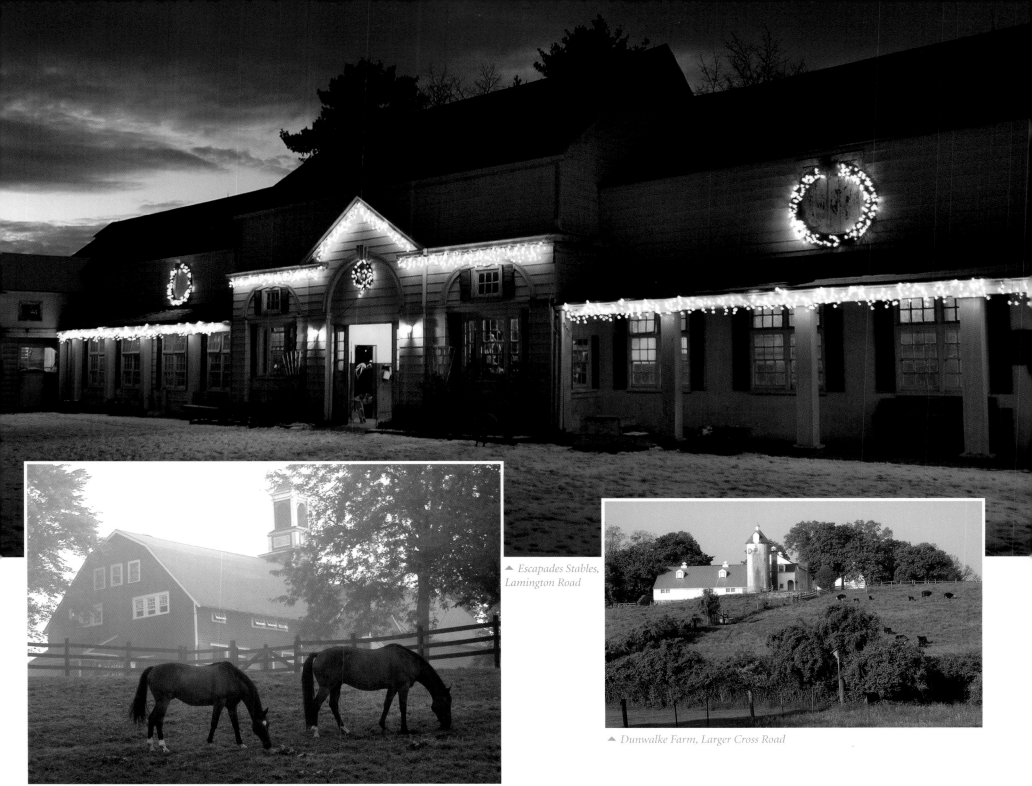

▲ Escapades Stables, Lamington Road

▲ Dunwalke Farm, Larger Cross Road

▲ Middlebrook Farm, Larger Cross Road   BEDMINSTER ∞ *17* ∞ Township

Bernards
Township

In the early 1700s John Harrison was employed by the East Jersey Proprietors to secure title for all Indian lands in the province. In 1717 Harrison secured a parcel of 3,000 acres from Lenape Chief Nowenoik, which was followed by a 7,000 acre purchase by William Penn. That same year, Scots-Irish settlers started the Presbyterian Church near an ancient white oak tree (today's Basking Ridge Oak). "Bernardston" Township was chartered in 1760 and named for Sir Francis Bernard, colonial governor of New Jersey. The township's rich Revolutionary history includes tales of Washington, Lafayette, Lord Stirling and Rochambeau. The railroad of the 1870s, as well as interstate highways of the 1970s, brought an influx of new residents to the area. Today Bernards Township is an upscale suburban community, home to corporations, historic village centers and parkland for all to enjoy.

▼ *Basking Ridge Presbyterian Church*

▲ *Lord Stirling Stables*

▲ *Blue Star Memorial Marker, Allen Street Gazebo*

◄ *Van Dorn Mill (1843), Franklin Corners Historic District*

▼ *Stonehouse Road*

Basking Ridge Oak, Basking Ridge Presbyterian Church Cemetery

▲ Sledding behind
The Chuch of Saint James

▶ Bernards Township Library

▲ Liberty Corner School

Ornamental archway at Lyons Train Station

Lyons Campus of the VA New Jersey Health Care System

Frothingham / Sloan House (1919), US Golf Association Museum

Revolutionary War Veteran marker, Basking Ridge Presbyterian Church Cemetery

Brick Academy (1809)

▲ Bernards Township
Community Center

▲ Crane Farm

▲ Olde Mill Inn sign, North Maple Avenue

Chabad Jewish Center
at Basking Ridge

▲ *13th Annual Charter Day Celebration,
Oak Street School Field*

◀ *Bernards Township Municipal Building*

Wildflowers,
Environmental Education Center
at Lord Stirling Park

Bernardsville

Borough

The northwestern section of Bernards Township was originally known as Vealtown. The Vealtown Tavern (today's Old Library) was a stopover for travelers on Morristown Road since the time of the Revolution. In 1840, Vealtown was renamed Bernardsville—honoring New Jersey colonial Governor, Sir Francis Bernard. After the Civil War, the area became a summer retreat for wealthy New Yorkers when the West Line Railroad was extended from Summit to Bernardsville in 1872. Through the 1890s, and into the early 20th century, grand estates were built creating the Bernardsville "Mountain Colony." Splitting from Bernards Township, Bernardsville became a borough in 1924, and continues to be the heart of Somerset Hills.

▼ *Bernardsville High School Track*

▲ *Horse trough, Claremont & Mendham Roads*

▼ *Bernards Inn and Millicent Fenwick Statue*

▲ *Bernardsville Public Library*

▶ *Old Library and historic marker*

▼ *Twin Lakes, Mount Harmony Road*

▲ *Mill pond spillway near Municipal Building*
◀ *Mill pond and Municipal Building*

▶ *Mine Brook near*
Our Lady of Perpetual Help Church

Millicent Fenwick Statue

▲ Bernardsville Farmers' Market

▼ Memorial Day Parade

▲ Jerolaman's General Store

▲ *Gardens near Train Station*
◀ *Gardens at Olcott Square*

Bound Brook

Borough

▶ Flags at Vosseller & West Union Avenues

Somerset County's first land grant was in 1681. Thomas Codrington, one of eight original proprietors who purchased land from the Lenape, later built his home along Bound Brook—a small tributary of the Raritan River, and called it "Rackawackhana." Flooding was common and growth was slow through the 1700s. During the Revolutionary War, Bound Brook was attacked by the British in 1777 and again raided in 1780. The town experienced growth through the 19th century due to the Swift-Sure Stage Line, the Delaware & Raritan Canal and the railroad. This growth led to Bound Brook's break from Bridgewater and it became a borough in 1891. Although most of the industry is now gone, Bound Brook remains a residential community with period homes and serves as a railroad hub for commuters.

▼ *Bound Brook Roundabout*

▲ *Queens Bridge over Raritan River*   ▶ *Brook Arts Center*

◀ *Bound Brook Memorial Library*

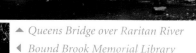

2007 Bound Brook Criterium

◄ Battle of Bound Brook reenactment

◄ The Old Presbyterian Graveyard

▲ *Bound Brook Farmers' Market, Train Station Parking Lot*

◀ *Strawberry Festival and Flea Market,*
Bound Brook United Methodist Church

▲ Main Street

▲ *The Presbyterian Church at Bound Brook (1896)*

Branchburg
Township

Bordering the Lamington River, as well as the North and South Branches of the Raritan River, Branchburg Township is aptly named. John Dobie's Plantation on Fairview Drive, served as an anchor point for the controversial 1687 Keith Line dividing East and West Jersey. The land originally inhabited by the Lenape, was purchased by the East Jersey Proprietors and settled by both the Dutch and English. Old York Road was a colonial pathway from New York to Philadelphia and the Swift-Sure Stage Line stopped midway at the White Oak Tavern in Branchburg. Partitioned from Bridgewater, Branchburg became a township in 1845. Today Branchburg remains a semi-rural community positioned between Routes 22 and 202. A one-room Victorian schoolhouse and preserved farmland are pleasant reminders of Branchburg's quaint agrarian past.

▼ *Lamington River near Burnt Mills Road*

▲ *North Branch*

◀ *South Branch School (1873)*

▶ *Branchburg Municipal Building*

▲ *South Branch Road*

▲ *South Branch Raritan River, view from Opie/River Road Bridge*

▲ *Holland Brook*

Balloons over Readington Road (New Jersey Festival of Ballooning)

◀ *Neshanic Station Farm,*
Home & Garden Center

▶ *Neshanic Flea Market*
and TJ's Luncheonette,
Neshanic Station

▲ *Opie Road*

▲ Ralph T. Reeve Cultural Center

▶ Andrew Ten Eyck House (ca. 1840s),
Branchburg Historical Society headquarters

Branchburg Recreation Department
and Branchburg Municipal Alliance
12th Annual Downhill Race

Neshanic Valley Golf Course

BRANCHBURG ⟷ *49* ⟷ Township

Raritan Valley Community College

Somerset County Cultural Diversity Coalition
26th Annual Somerset County International Festival
at Raritan Valley Community Colllege

Bridgewater
Township

Named for Bridgewater in Somerset, England, this township was created by Royal Charter of King George II in 1749. The land was originally purchased from the Lenape by the East Jersey Proprietors in the late 1600s. As one of the initial 104 townships of New Jersey incorporated in 1798, Bridgewater formerly included today's Warren and Branchburg Townships, as well as Bound Brook, Raritan and Somerville. Revolutionary history is reenacted each year on the 4th of July at Middlebrook Encampment, where the first American flag flew over the Continental Army. Bridgewater Township is an affluent suburban community with a thriving corporate and economic center and is located at the crossroads of Somerset County.

◀ *Red-tailed Hawk,*
▼ *Chimney Rock,*
Washington Valley Park

▼ *Bridgewater Commons Mall*

▼ *Ardmaer Park,*
Bradley Gardens

▲ *Milltown School*

◀ *Railroad bridge,*
North Branch Raritan River

◇◇◇ 52 ◇◇◇

▶ *Finderne Fire Department*

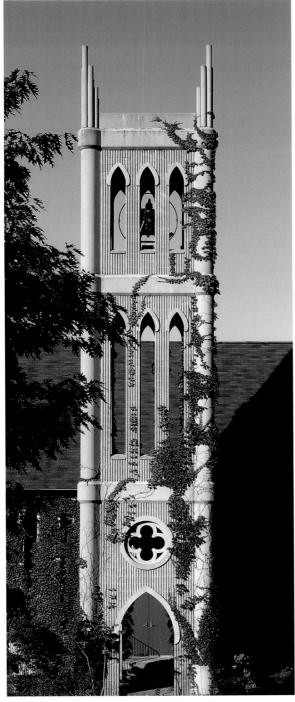

▲ *St. Martin's Episcopal Church, Martinsville*

▲ *Sri Venkateswara Temple (Balaji Mandir)*

*60th Annual
Somerset County 4-H Fair,
North Branch Park*

Somerset Patriots game,
Commerce Bank Ballpark

Sunset Lake

▲ Virginia Bluebells,
Duke Island Park

◀ 8th Annual Party in The Park,
Duke Island Park

▲ Van Veghten House (mid-1700s)

▲ Van Horne House (mid-1700s)

◀ "General George Washington"
at Middlebrook Encampment

▲ *Van Horne House, decorated by Gardeners of Somerset Valley*

Far Hills

Borough

Although settled since the mid-1700s, it was the railroad's expansion to the Somerset Hills in 1870 which led to the area's discovery by wealthy New York businessmen. Real estate broker, Evander H. Schley, purchased thousands of acres of farmland in Bernards Township in the 1880s and began selling country estate properties. In 1899, Schley and David Dumont offered lots of a subdivision called Dumont Farm which would later become Far Hills village. In 1921, the Borough of Far Hills was partitioned from Bernards Township. Far Hills is host to the Far Hills Race Meeting, weekend cricket matches at the Fairgrounds and the semiannual VNA Rummage Sale.

▼ *Memorial Day Parade*

▼ *Dumont Road*

▲ *Moorland Farms*

▶ *Memorial Day, Veterans Memorial*

▲ *Visiting Nurse Association of Somerset Hills Spring Rummage Sale*

Ravine Lake Dam

▲ Tony Nervine, Far Hills Barber Shop

▲ Pete Welsh, Team Welsh Jeep/Chrysler

▲ Jack Turpin, Turpin Real Estate

▲ *Millennium Cricket League, Far Hills Fairgrounds*

▶ *Aerial (Far Hills Race Meeting)*

Music at Moorland, Somerset Medical Center Foundation

Franklin
Township

Located in the southeastern corner of the county, the area was settled by the Dutch in the 1650s and was formed as the Eastern Precinct around 1745. Franklin Township was probably named after Benjamin Franklin and was incorporated as one of the initial 104 townships of New Jersey in 1798. Revolutionary War sites are found along Kings Highway—today's Route 27, and also at Rockingham, which was moved to the township from Rocky Hill in 1897. The Delaware and Raritan Canal, built in 1834, was a major development for Franklin Township where a 22-mile stretch runs from Kingston to New Brunswick. Fortunately, the Canal has been preserved as parkland. Franklin Township is Somerset County's most populous municipality and second largest in area.

▶ *Six Mile Run*
Reformed Church (1879)

◀ *Griggstown*

▲ *Aerial (Somerset Christian College, Zarephath)*

▼ *War Memorial, Franklin Municipal Complex*

▶ *Shree Swaminarayan*
Mandir Vadtal Dham

▲ Van Wickle House (1722)

▼ Blackwells Mills Canal House (1835)

▲ Wyckoff-Garretson House (1730)

▲ Hageman Farm Horse Barn (1876)

Historic properties
preserved and restored by
The Meadows Foundation
[both pages]

▲ Van Liew-Suydam House (1875)

Rudolf W. van der Goot Rose Garden, Colonial Park Arboretum

▲ Rudolf W. van der Goot Rose Garden, Colonial Park Arboretum

◀ ▼ *5th Annual Asian-American Heritage Festival, Ukrainian Cultural Center*

▲ *Love & Peace Rose*

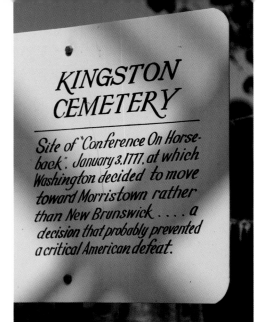

KINGSTON CEMETERY

Site of "Conference On Horse-back", January 3, 1777, at which Washington decided to move toward Morristown rather than New Brunswick.....a decision that probably prevented a critical American defeat.

▲ ▶ *Kingston Presbyterian Church Cemetery*

◀ ▲ *Kingston Bridge (1798)*

Rockingham (George Washington's last military headquarters)   FRANKLIN ∞ *75* ∞ Township

▲ *Hamilton Street*
Cruise Night,
Nora's Shopping Center

◀ *Franklin Township*
Summer Child Care Program
Car Wash Fundraiser

First Annual Bocce Invitational at Colonial Park   FRANKLIN ∞ 77 ∞ Township   *(Fundraiser benefitting Operation Shoebox New Jersey)*

Green Brook
Township

Stretching from the plains of the Raritan River to the first Watchung Mountain, the area was home to the Raritan tribe of the Lenape and Chief Metapes—a signatory of many of the Indian purchases by the East Jersey Proprietors in the late 1600s. The first settlers were Quakers who arrived in the early 1700s. During the Revolution the "Blue Hills" played a vital role, offering a 60-mile vantage point to George Washington and his generals who monitored the movements of the British in the valley below. The "Rock" was commemorated in 1913 by creation of Washington Rock State Park. Originally established as North Plainfield Township, the municipality was subdivided from Warren Township in 1872 and officially renamed Green Brook Township in 1932. Commercial enterprises now line Route 22, while residential neighborhoods are found on the ridge and valley.

▶ *Washington Rock State Park*

▼ ▲ *Aerial views*

▲ *Green Brook*

▼ *Cardinal Lane, Washington Rock State Park*

CARDINAL LANE

Built in the mid-1800's for stagecoach access, Cardinal Lane was used to shuttle tourists between the Plainfield Railway Station and Washington Rock.

Washington Rock State Park

GREEN BROOK ᴖᴖ *79* ᴖᴖᴖTownship

9 - 11
NEVER
FORGET

GREEN BROOK TOWNSHIP
SEPTEMBER 11, 2001
MEMORIAL
TRAGICALLY LOST
LOVINGLY REMEMBERED
DEDICATED SEPTEMBER 11, 2005

▲ *Greenbrook Road*

◄ ▲ *Green Brook Township 9/11 Memorial*
Garden of Remembrance, Top of the World Park

▲ Green Brook Middle School

▲ Green Brook Fire Department

▲ Green Brook Township Municipal Building

Eateries along Route 22

▲ *Rose's Evergreen,*
Route 22

◀ ▲ *Rawhide Rescue's Four-legged Fitness Walk, Top of The World Way*

Hillsborough
Township

The Unami tribe of the Lenape lived in the area for thousands of years before the Dutch settlers arrived in the mid-1600s. Hillsborough, created by Royal Charter in 1771, from portions of the Western Precinct, was organized as one of the original townships of New Jersey in 1798. Early landowners included William Penn and Peter Sonmans. During the Revolution it was a pathway for General Washington as he moved north from Princeton. Encompassing over 50 square miles, Hillsborough is the largest municipalty of the county. The township is home to Duke Farms, the former estate of James Buchanan Duke, and Duke Gardens, created in the 1960s by heiress Doris Duke. With an agricultural past and numerous historic villages, Hillsborough is a popular suburban community and was recently mentioned as one of "The Best Places to Live" by *Money* magazine.

▶ *USGS flood gauge, Millstone River*

▶ *Dutch barn, Millstone Valley Agricultural Historic District*

▼ *Duke Farms*

▶ *Hillsborough Post Office*

United States
Post Office

Hillsborough, NJ 08844

▲ *Neshanic Garden Club
planting Sensory Garden,
Ann Van Middlesworth Park*

◀ *Italian Garden,
Duke Gardens*

Annual Youth Fishing Derby, Sourland Mountain Preserve

▲ *Farm, Zion Road*
◀ *Sunhaven Farms, Orchard Drive*

▲ *Independence Day Celebration*

▶ *27th Annual Hillsborough Firemen's Fair*

▼ Community Playground, Hillsborough Municipal Complex

◀ Somerset Valley YMCA
7th Annual Hillsborough Hop 5K Race

▼ Grand Marshal, Captain Becky Lapidow,
Memorial Day Ceremonies

▲ Memorial Day Parade

▲ *Hillsborough Little League Willow Road Complex (Opening Day)*

▼ *Alzheimer's Association 20th Annual Polo Classic, Hillsborough Country Club*

▲ *Hillsborough Municipal Complex Soccer Fields*

▲ *Aerial (South Branch Historic District, Sourland Mountain)*

◀ ▲ ▲ ▶
South Branch Reformed Church
Chicken Barbeque

▲ Aerial (Neshanic Reformed Church, Amwell Road)

▲ Clover Hill Reformed Church (1834)

Manville
Borough

Located near the junction of the Millstone and Raritan Rivers, the area was first settled by the Dutch in the mid-1600s. It was originally part of Hillsborough Township and was organized as a borough in 1929. Manville was named for the Johns-Manville Corporation– the world's largest asbestos manufacturer, which established a factory here in 1912. Immigrants, mostly from Poland and Eastern Europe, became laborers in the factory. The Church of the Sacred Heart was founded in 1915 to serve this community of Catholic immigrants. Johns-Manville thrived through New Jersey's golden age of industry until its asbestos-related bankruptcy in 1982. Wholesale and retail commerce has replaced the industy and Manville remains a quiet residential community with a strong sense of patriotism and community pride.

▼ *Aerial*

▼ *Manville High School sign*

▼ *Manville Water Tower*

▲ *The Church of Christ The King*

▶ *Manville High School Marching Band, Memorial Day Parade*

Raritan River, Dukes Parkway

◀ *Manville VFW Post 2290 Ladies Auxiliary,
Memorial Day Parade*

◀ ▲ *Manville VFW Post 2290,
Memorial Day Services*

ADESA New Jersey (vehicle auction)

HIGHLAND PARK PUBLIC LIBRARY

Businesses on Main Street

*Sacred Heart Church
39th Annual Summer Festival*

Millstone

Borough

The smallest municipality of Somerset County, Millstone, previously known as Somerset Courthouse, was the second county seat from 1738 until the British raid in 1779. British Major John Simcoe and the Queens Rangers freed prisoners being held there and afterwards burned the court house and jail. Somerset Court House was strategically located along the Millstone River at the crossroads of colonial routes. Originally part of Hillsborough Township, the area was occupied by the Lenape and later settled by the Dutch in the late 1600s. The Old Millstone Forge Museum commemorates the oldest Blacksmith Shop in the country. The Delaware and Raritan Canal brought new growth in the 19th century, leading to Millstone's incorporation as a borough in 1894. Today Millstone is a quiet village with a Historic District that includes 58 buildings.

▸ *Millstone Borough Hall (1860)*

▴ *Historic millstone at Hillsborough Reformed Church*
◂ *Hillsborough Reformed Church Cemetery*

▸ *Historic marker commemorating
Revolutionary War site of the
burning of Somerset Court House*

Hillsborough Reformed Church at Millstone (1828)

▲ ▶ *18th Annual Town-wide Yard Sale*

◀ *John Van Doren House (1752)*

◄ ▲ *Blacksmith, Ben Suhaka*

▲ *Old Millstone Forge Blacksmith Shop and Museum*

Montgomery
Township

Originally occupied by the Lenape, this area was part of the Western Precinct and settled by the Dutch and English in the early 1700s. Montgomery was incorporated in 1798 and included Princeton and Rocky Hill, which were partitioned from it in the 1800s. It was named in honor of Revolutionary War General Richard Montgomery who died in the Battle of Quebec in 1775. Montgomery Township is located in the southern portion of Somerset County, positioned between the Millstone River and the Sourland Mountain. It had remained agricultural through the 20th century and has now become a desirable residential community with one of the highest-ranking school districts in the state.

▼ *Aerial (Pike Run Road, Reid Avenue, Boice Lane and Hudnut Lane)*

◀ *Country Club Drive*

▼ *Skillman Road & Belle Mead-Blawenburg Road*

▲ *Mill Pond Bridge (1820s) and dam (2000)*

∞∞∞ *104* ∞∞∞

Bedens Brook Bridge [Opossum Road Bridge] (1822)

Blawenburg Band, started in 1890

(Conductor Jerry Rife with some band members)

Blawenburg Reformed Church (1830)

Mill Pond, Bridgepoint Historic District

▲ *Montgomery Center for the Arts*
at the 1860 House

◀ *Lucy Graves-McVicker,*
Artist in Residence

MONTGOMERY ∞ 110 ∞ Township

Montgomery High School
Graduation
June 21, 2007

▲ *Gazebo, Harlingen*

▲ *Dirck Gulick House (1752)*

▲ *Harlingen Church (1851)*

▲ *Harlingen Road Bridge Over Fox Brook (1890)*

North Plainfield
Borough

Originally part of Warren Township, then partitioned in 1872 as North Plainfield Township, the Borough of North Plainfield was further sub-divided in 1885. Positioned at the base of the first Watchung Mountain and bordered by the Green Brook, North Plainfield was known as "Blue Hills" and centered on the Cornelius Vermeule plantation. The Victorian-era Van Deventer-Brunson House was built near the original Vermeule Dutch homestead. By the mid-1800s the railroad had reached the Plainfields, and in the 1920s State Route 29 (today's Route 22) was built. These events brought new residents who built country estates and transitioned North Plainfield from rural to suburban.

▼ St. Joseph Church

▶ North Plainfield Municipal Building

▼ Somerset Street & Greenbrook Road

▶ North Plainfield Exempts Fire Museum

Van Deventer-Brunson House (Vermeule Mansion)   NORTH PLAINFIELD ∞ *115* ∞ Township

Washington Park Historic District

▲ West End School

▲ North Plainfield High School

▶ Cheerleaders, North Plainfield High School

Community Day and
North Plainfield Lions
Chili Cookoff

GRAND MARSHALLS
Karlie Moss
Deep Goraya

July 4th Parade

Peapack-Gladstone
Borough

Located in the hills of the Highlands, Peapack and Gladstone were two villages within Bedminster Township that joined together as a single entity and incorporated as a borough in 1912. Dr. John Johnstone and George Willocks first purchased the land from the East Jersey Proprietors in 1701—a transaction known as the "Peapack Patent." The villages experienced growth in the late 1800s when the railroad was extended from Bernardsville. In 1895 "Blairsden," the Beaux-Arts mansion of Clinton Ledyard Blair, was built on the mountaintop overlooking the North Branch Raritan River. Today Peapack-Gladstone maintains an upscale rural charm while also being home to major corporations and the Matheny Medical and Education Center.

▲ Blairsden

▲ St. Brigid Church

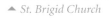
▼ Liberty Pond

▲ Lime Kiln Park

▶ Peapack Reformed Church

*Peapack-Gladstone
Community Day
at Liberty Park*

▲ *Raritan River, Natirar*

◀ *Ladd Mansion, Natirar*

▲ *Pfizer*

◀ *Gladstone Train Station*

Peapack Reformed Church (1872)

Raritan
Borough

Settled in 1683 by the Dutch, Raritan Town was carved from Bridgewater Township in 1868 and eventually was allowed to become an independent borough in 1948. Raritan borders the Raritan River–both were named after the Naraticong Tribe of Lenape that inhabited the area. Raritan is located at the crossroads of Routes 28, 202 and 206 (the Somerville Circle) and the Route 202 overpass was named in honor of Raritan's legendary World War II hero, John Basilone. The town also honors his memory with a monument and annual parade. The railroad station, built in1895, continues to serve local commuters of the Raritan Valley Line.

▼ *John Basilone Monument*

▼ *River Park at Raritan*

▼ *Raritan Train Station*

▲ *Aerial (John Basilone Memorial Bridge over Somerville Circle)*

Nevius Street Bridge and Lyman Street Bridge, Raritan River

◀ ▲ *St. Ann's Parish, Saint Rocco Processional*

▼ *Third Reformed Church (1851)*

25th Annual
John Basilone Memorial Parade

▲ Uncle Vinnie's Clam Bar
◀ Pat Chiaffarano, Frame Me

▲ *Raritan Public Library, The General John Frelinghuysen House (ca. early 1700s)*

▲ *Raritan Relief Hose Company #2*

Rocky Hill

Borough

Rocky Hill's history dates from the early 1700s when mills (some owned by John Hart, signer of the Declaration of Independence) were in operation on the Millstone River. General Washington passed through Rocky Hill on his escape from Princeton in 1777 and returned again in 1783, staying at the Berrien Mansion, "Rockingham," which served as his final headquarters where he authored his Farewell Address to the Army. Originally part of Montgomery Township, Rocky Hill became an independent borough in 1890. The town flourished in the 1800s into the early 1900s due to the railroad, the Delaware & Raritan Canal and the Excelsior Terra Cotta factory. Today the Rocky Hill Historic District includes over 100 structures.

▼ *Rocky Hill Cemetery*

▼ *Trinity Episcopal Church of Rocky Hill (1862)*

▲ *First Reformed Church of Rocky Hill (1856)*

▲ *Rocky Hill Buy the Cup*

▶ *Rocky Hill Municipal Building*

John Shedd Designs

▲ Mary Jacobs Memorial Library

▶ Helen "Mei Mei" Morris
Library Director

Somerville
Borough

Dutch settlers from Long Island arrived here in 1683 and purchased land from the Lenape. The settlement, called Raritan, was later renamed Somerville by the English and was part of Bridgewater Township. Philadelphia merchant John Wallace completed his "Hope Farm" there in 1776 which was leased to George Washington in the winter of 1778-1779. The Elizabeth and Somerville Railroad was chartered in 1831 and reached Somerville in 1842. Somerville was formed as a town within Bridgewater in 1863 and later incorporated as an independent borough in 1909. Somerset County's white marble court house was also completed in 1909 and Somerville has served as the third county seat since 1782. With Victorian-era architecture, Main Street restaurants, County offices and the Somerset Medical Center, Somerville is truly the heart of Somerset County.

◀ *Somerville Train Station*

▶ *John Haynes Lord Memorial Fountain (1909)*

▼ *"Dixietime" peforms at Borough Hall lawn*

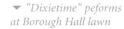

▲ *East High Street bridge, Peter's Brook Greenway*   ▶ *Hotel Somerset*

Somerville Borough Hall (1888)

The clock tower bears the inscription **TIME TO REMEMBER**.

Somerset County 9/11 Memorial

Wallace House (1775-1776)

Old Dutch Parsonage (1751)

James Kurzenberger, Director of
Wallace House & Old Dutch Parsonage

▲ Somerville Cruise Night

▲ Somerville Street Fair

▼ St. Patrick's Day Parade

◀ Immaculata High School
5K Race For Freedom

The Tour of Somerville
(presented by Middle Earth)

▼ *Somerville Senior Housing*

▲ ▶ *Altamont Place*

Somerville Fire Department Museum

▲ *West Main & Maple Streets*

▶ *Dr. Kathleen C. Toomey,*
The Steeplechase Cancer Center,
Somerset Medical Center

South Bound Brook
Borough

In 1681, Englishman John Inian purchased a large tract of land south of the Raritan River near Bound Book. He later sold it to William Dockwra, who subdivided it into smaller plantation lots. The Abraham Staats House was built on one these plantations around 1740. The house later became the Revolutionary War headquarters of Baron Von Steuben. The area was involved in the Battle of Bound Brook in 1777. South Bound Brook was formed as a town within Franklin Township (with a temporary name change to "Bloomington" in the mid-1800s). The town grew prosperous due to the arrival of the Delaware & Raritan Canal in 1834 and it became an independent borough in 1907. The Ukrainian Orthodox Church of America is headquartered in South Bound Brook. Today South Bound Brook boasts "small town" appeal with a historic past.

▼ *South Battlefield, D&R Canal State Park*

▼ *Reformed Church of South Bound Brook (1846)*

▶ *Main Street & Von Steuben Lane*

▲ *Borough Hall*   ▶ *Robert Morris School*

South Bound Brook sign

Hendrick Fisher Homestead (1688)

◀ St. Andrew Memorial Church,
Ukrainian Orthodox Church of the United States of America

▲ *D&R Canal Lock 11*

▲ *Aerial (Downtown and D&R Canal)*

Warren
Township

Extending from the ridge of the First Watchung Mountain, northward across the Second Watchung Mountain to the Passaic and Dead Rivers, this lush mountain land was sparsely inhabited by the Lenape before European settlers arrived in the early 1720s. The area was originally part of Essex County until 1743 when the borders of Somerset County were redefined. Warren Township was later divided from Bernards and Bridgewater Townships and incorporated in 1806. Warren was named in honor of Revolutionary General Joseph Warren—killed at the Battle of Bunker Hill. The township remained sparsely populated through mid-20th century. It was not until 1986, when Route 78 was completed, that the township experienced its greatest growth. The remaining farms gave way to corporate centers and residential developments. Downtown Warrenville is the township's commercial center located along Washington Valley Road.

▼ *Warren Court and Veterans Memorial*

▲ *Country Gentleman Farm Market*

▼ *Warrenbrook Senior Center*

▲ *Mt. Horeb United Methodist Church*

▶ *Watchung Hills Elks Lodge 2252*

*Mt. Bethel Baptist
Meetinghouse (1757)*

Kirch-Ford
Homestead (ca. 1750)

WARREN TOWNSHIP
MIDDLE SCHOOL
BAND

Memorial Day Parade

Memorial Day Parade

MT. BETHEL VOL FIRE CO NO. 1
ORGANIZED 1911

FORD MODEL 1928 HOWE H B 5
A A

FIRST PUMPER
WARREN TOWNSHIP N. J.

RAVE-UP

▲ *Warren Girls Softball,*
Warren Municipal Fields

◀ *Watchung Hills*
Regional High School

Watchung
Borough

Located at the eastern edge of Somerset County, Watchung was named after the Lenape word for "High Hills." The area was also known as Browestown and Washingtonville. It was partitioned from North Plainfield Township (which was earlier divided from Warren Township) and incorporated as a borough in 1926. The Lenape inhabited the area when the Dutch arrived in 1670. The Washingtonville dam. built in the late1800s, created Watchung Lake. Wilson's Pond (Best Lake) was also created in the 1800s. Today, Watchung is an upscale residential community nestled in the hills surrounding the lakes. Watchung's commercial area, including the Blue Star Shopping Center, is found along Route 22.

◄ *Watchung sign near Best Lake*

▼ *Municipal Building*

▶ *Mount Saint Mary Academy*

▲ *War memorials, Watchung Circle*

▶ *Watchung Arts Center*

WATCHUNG ARTS CENTER

▲ *Orange Mountain Basalt near Municipal Building*

▲ *The Mary E. Wilson Memorial Chapel*

Best Lake

▲ *Watchung Fire Department*

▲ *Watchung Library*

▲ *Blue Star Shopping Center*

Watchung Lake

Aesthetic Press used this book as a fundraiser benefitting:

The Wellness Community of Central New Jersey

The Wellness Community of Central New Jersey is part of an international nonprofit organization devoted solely to providing emotional support, education and hope to people living with cancer. Its mission is to help people affected by cancer enhance their health and well-being in a safe, supportive, home-like environment.

Located in Bedminster and easily accessible to those who reside or work in central New Jersey, our programs are free of charge. Individuals come to The Wellness Community at any time during their cancer journey—at diagnosis, in treatment and into survivorship. All services are offered to people with cancer and their caregivers. Programs are also offered for children whose parents have cancer.

The Wellness Community of Central New Jersey programs include professionally facilitated support groups, networking groups for people with specific types of cancer, educational workshops, healthy cooking demonstrations, nutrition classes, light exercise activities, stress management sessions, lectures by experts in the field of oncology—all with laughter, joy and hope—

...because no one should face cancer alone.

**The Wellness Community
of Central New Jersey**
3 Crossroads Drive
Bedminster NJ 07921

Telephone: 908-658-5400
www.thewellnesscommunity.org/cnj

WALTER CHOROSZEWSKI

Since 1981 Walter Choroszewski has been promoting a positive image of New Jersey through his photographic creativity and has published numerous wall calendars and coffee-table books about the state. Walter's photographs were used to launch the popular "New Jersey & You" state tourism campaign of the 1980s and he was its primary photographer for almost two decades. His images of the state have been featured in advertising campaigns, corporate annual reports, on telephone directory covers and magazine covers.

Choroszewski is a photographer, graphic artist, designer and videographer. He also enjoys speaking to school children and various adult groups. For over 20 years he has been encouraging pride in New Jersey through his popular presentation, "New Jersey, Celebrate Your State."

Walter and his wife, Susan, live in the Historic District of South Branch in Hillsborough Township.

SOURCES & ACKNOWLEDGEMENTS

Although I have a passion for history, I am not a historian, nor an expert on Somerset County. The foreword and community profiles were based on the writings of many other individuals, and I wish to thank them for their invaluable contributions which aided me in writing for this publication.

My research was accomplished through internet-based resources. Every effort has been made to include all reference sources; however, there is a chance that errors and omissions may have occurred. I apologize to any parties I have omitted and will gladly credit them in future editions.

The starting point for my research was the official County of Somerset website, co.somerset.nj.us, which offered a link to each municipality's website. These websites include: bedminster.us; bernards.org; bernardsvilleboro.org; boundbrooknj.net; branchburg.nj.us; bridgewaternj.gov; franklintwpnj.org; greenbrooktwp.org; hillsborough-nj.org; millstoneboro.org; twp.montgomery.nj.us; northplainfield.org; peapack-gladstone-nj.gov; raritanboro.org; somervillenj.org; warrennj.org; watchungnj.com.

Other internet resources include: books.google.com (Centennial History of Somerset County [New Jersey] by Abraham Messler, 1878); books.google.com (Tracts and other papers relating principally to the origin, settlement, and progress of the colonies in North America by Peter Force, 1836); getnj.com (Historic Roadsides of New Jersey [Somerset County] by The Society of Colonial Wars in the State of New Jersey, 1928); c-n.com (Courier News Online – Your Towns: Somerset County [Central Jersey Living Guide]); historicalsocietyofsomersethills.org; memory.loc.gov (The George Washington Papers at the Library of Congress); njchurchscape.com; njfreeways.com; njskylands.com; sacred-heart-church.org; somersetcountyparks.org; state.nj.us (Using the Records of East and West Jersey Proprietors by Joseph R. Klett, 2006); westjerseyhistory.org. An especially useful resource was: wikipedia.org.

I also used internet resources to monitor events in the county including: c-n.com (Courier News); nj.com/events (Star-Ledger); nj.com/reporter/events (The Reporter / Somerset); princetonol.com/events (Princeton Online).

On a personal level, I would like to express my sincere gratitude and appreciation to all who have assisted me in this endeavor. First and foremost, I would like to thank my wife and business partner, Susan Choroszewski, for her behind-the-scenes involvement in almost every aspect of the book. As always, I appreciate Debbie Lavell, our office manager, for her meticulous clerical support. I am also grateful to Eunice Jadlocki, Executive Director of The Wellness Community of Central New Jersey, for her friendship and for her belief and support of this project; and to Patricia Lunny, Marketing/Outreach Director of The Wellness Community of Central New Jersey for her gallant efforts with this fundraiser.

Confluence of North and South Branch Raritan Rivers, Branchburg